CALAVERA
Abecedario
A Day of the Dead Alphabet Book

JEANETTE WINTER

Clarion Books
An Imprint of HarperCollins*Publishers*
Boston New York
Printed in China

On a rooftop patio in Mexico City,
the *calaveras* come to life.

Like his father before him,
Don Pedro makes skeletons
for the *fiesta* of *el Día de los Muertos.*

Enrique,

Felipe,

and Miguel

help their father
make the *calaveras* with torn pieces
of brown paper and wheat paste.

Don Pedro wraps paste-covered paper around bamboo.

Enrique, Felipe, and Miguel

press paste-covered paper into molds.

The sun dries the paper.

Then Don Pedro and his sons fasten the pieces
together with more paper and paste.

The *calaveras* are coming to life.

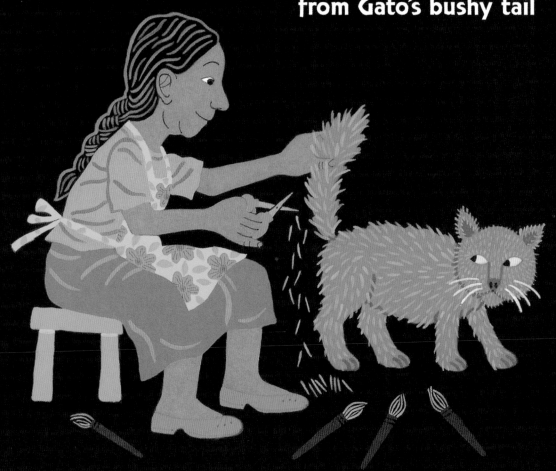

**Doña Adela snips hair
from Gato's bushy tail**

and makes brushes to paint the *calaveras.*

The years pile on top of one another.
Before long the sons are fathers.

Now Leonardo,   Ricardo,   and David help

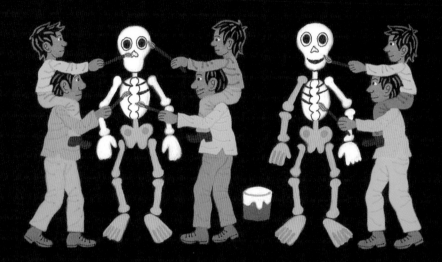

Enrique,   Felipe,   and Miguel.

And they all help
Don Pedro make
the *calaveras.*

The *fiesta* is coming soon. Fathers and sons and grandsons work into the night. The *calaveras* must be ready to dance on *el Día de los Muertos.*

At dawn on *fiesta* day,
the *calaveras* go to market.

And among the marigolds, candles, and
sugar skulls, the dance begins.

ÁNGEL

BRUJA

CANDELERA

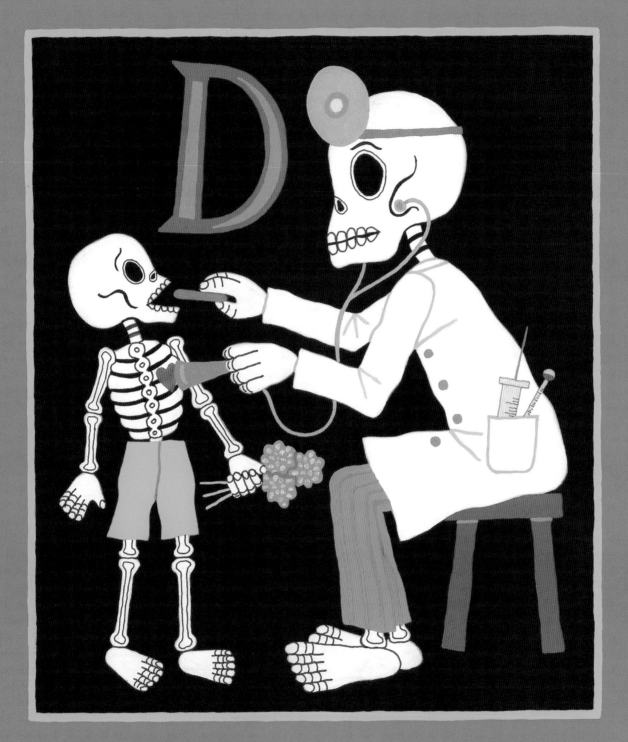

DOCTOR

ENFERMERA

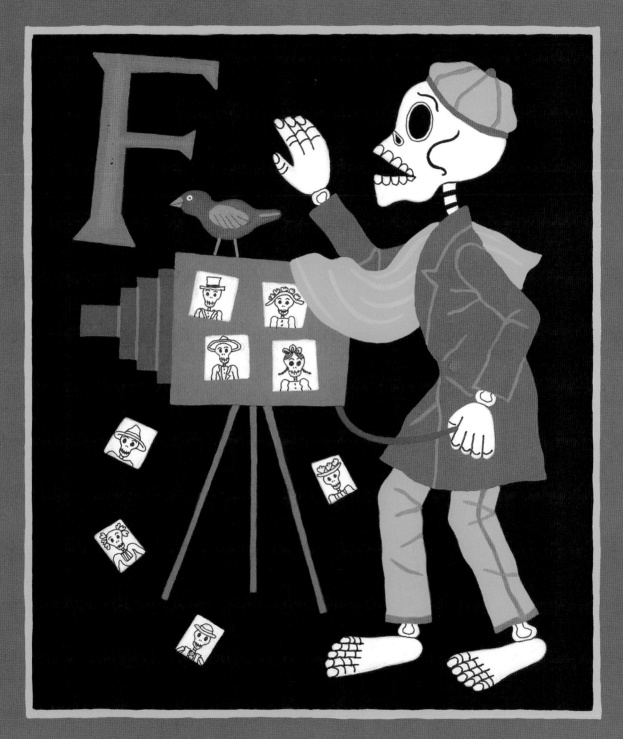

FOTÓGRAFO

GRANJERO

HUEVERA

ILUSTRADORA

JARDINERO

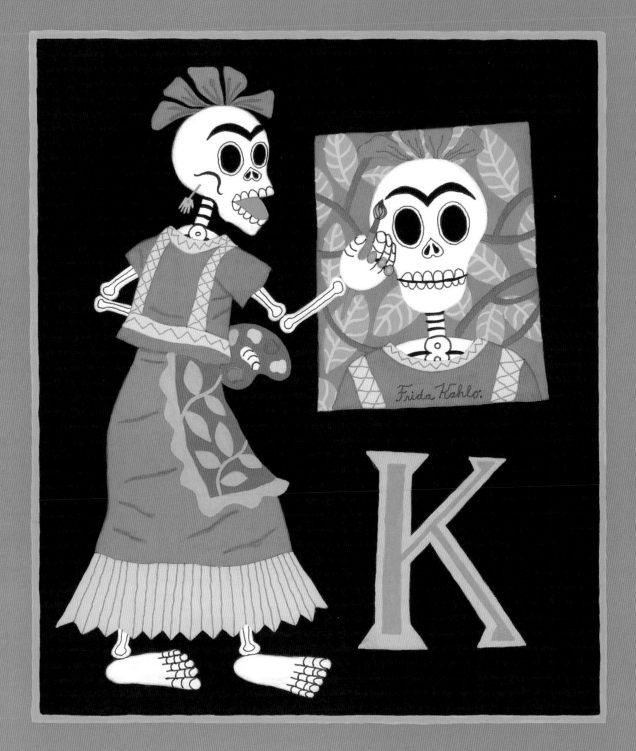

KAHLO

LIMONERA   LIMERA

MARIACHI

NOVIO   NOVIA

ORGANILLERO

PESCADORA

QUÍMICO

REY   REINA

SOMBRERERO

TORTILLERA

UNICORNIO

VAQUERO

XILOFONISTA

YUCA

ZAPATERO

Now the *fiesta* is over.
The dance is done.
The candles are out.

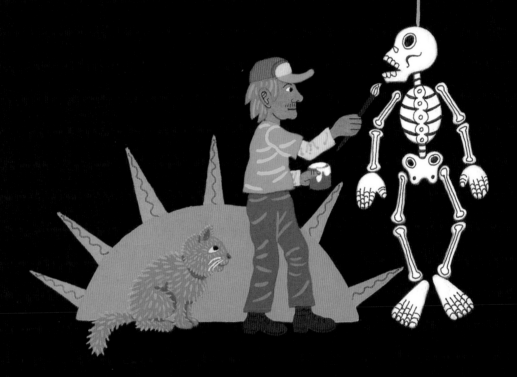

But when the morning sun lights the sky,
Don Pedro and his sons and grandsons
will begin again—making *calaveras* to
dance in the *fiesta* next year.

Alphabet Glossary

ángel	angel
bruja	witch
candelera	candlemaker
doctor	doctor
enfermera	nurse
fotógrafo	photographer
granjero	farmer
huevera	egg seller
ilustradora	illustrator
jardinero	gardener
Kahlo	Frida Kahlo Mexican painter (1907–1954)
limera	lime seller
limonera	lemon seller
mariachi	musician
novia	bride
novio	groom

organillero	organ-grinder
pescadora	fishmonger
químico	chemist
reina	queen
rey	king
sombrerero	hat maker
tortillera	tortilla maker
unicornio	unicorn
vaquero	cowboy
w	*
xilofonista	xylophonist
yuca	yucca
zapatero	shoemaker

* There are various interpretations of the Spanish alphabet,
which differs slightly from the English one illustrated in this book.
Many references indicate there is no *w*, and *ch*, *ll*, *ñ*, and *rr*
are often considered separate single letters.

AUTHOR'S NOTE

Mexico is a country of *fiestas*, and temporary *fiesta* markets are held everywhere throughout the year. The markets bloom with flowers, food, crafts, and papier-mâché creations in many forms: masks that are worn during the pre-Lenten *Carnaval*; giant firecracker-lined Judas figures that are ignited during *Semana Santa* (Holy Week); *piñatas* that are filled with toys and candy during *la Navidad* (Christmas); and *calaveras* that brighten *el Día de los Muertos* (Day of the Dead).

Don Pedro Linares, the man whose life inspired this story, learned to make papier-mâché objects, or *cartonería*, from his father. Don Pedro had skills so outstanding that his *cartonería*—especially his *calaveras*—became famous all over Mexico.

Since Don Pedro's death in 1992 at age eighty-six, his sons and grandsons have carried on the tradition of his art.

For Judythe Sieck

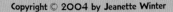

clarionbooks.com

For information about Don Pedro, the Linares family, and their colorful artwork, the author gratefully
acknowledges *En Calavera: The Papier-Mâché Art of the Linares Family* by Susan N. Masuoka,
published by the Fowler Museum of Cultural History at the University of California, Los Angeles.

Library of Congress Cataloging-in-Publication Data
Winter, Jeanette.
Calavera abecedario: a Day of the Dead alphabet book/Jeanette Winter.
p. cm.
1. All Souls' Day—Mexico. 2. Mexico—Social life and customs. I. Title.
GT 4995.A 4 W 56   2004
394.266'0972—dc 22   2004001554
ISBN 978-0-15-205110-5
ISBN 978-0-15-205906-4 pb

22 SCP 25 24 23 22 21 20 19 18

The illustrations in this book were done in acrylics and pen on Strathmore Bristol paper.
The display and text type were set in Neuland Medium.
Color separations by Bright Arts Ltd., Hong Kong
Printed by RR Donnelley, China
Production supervision by Ginger Boyer
Designed by Judythe Sieck